Let's Find the Fish

To Parents: This activity exercises your child's observational skills. If your child gets confused because the colors and patterns of the fish are different, remind him or her that there are many different kinds of fish in the world. The stickers for this activity can be found at the front of the book.

Sticker

Place  stickers on the fish.

Let's Find the Rabbits

To Parents: The rabbits on this page are different colors and shapes. Make sure your child understands that, despite these differences, they are all the same type of animal.

GOOD JOB!
Sticker

Place  stickers on the rabbits.

Let's Trace Straight Lines

To Parents: Make sure your child draws from the top to the bottom. This skill will come in handy as she or he begins to draw letters and numbers.

The animals are watching the rain. Trace the lines from ★ to ⬤ to make the rain fall.

4

Let's Draw Straight Lines

To Parents: Have your child start drawing at the end of each string. He or she will begin by following the dotted line to connect the string to the animal's hand. Then, your child will draw the extra string without following a dotted line. Ask your child, "What color balloon is the cat holding?"

GOOD JOB!

Sticker

The animals want to hold the balloons. Finish drawing the strings so they reach each animal's hand.

Let's Draw Straight Lines

To Parents: Being able to draw straight lines is an important step toward writing numbers and letters. Make sure your child draws each line in one stroke. Offer encouragement as your child draws.

Draw lines from ● to ●.

Let's Find the Number in the Fish

To Parents: In this activity, your child will practice recognizing numbers.

Find the number ^{ONE} 1 and color it using any color you like.

Let's Trace and Write Numbers

To Parents: Have your child trace the number with his or her finger first. Then he or she can practice tracing with a crayon.

Trace the number ^ONE **|** with your finger.

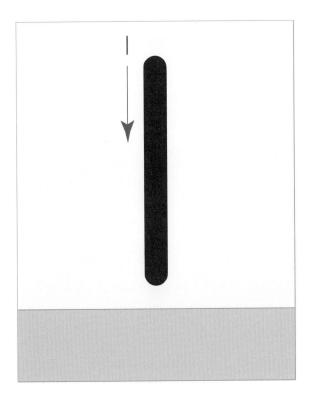

Trace the number ^ONE **|** with a crayon.

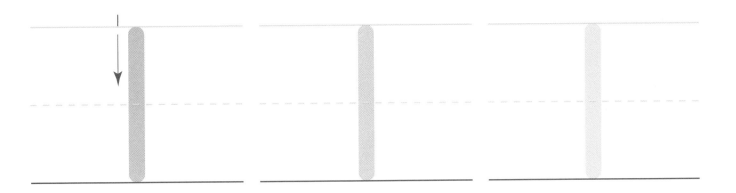

Let's Trace Horizontal Lines

To Parents: Guide your child to follow the dotted line with his or her finger. Then have your child trace the line with a crayon. Drawing horizontal lines will help prepare your child for writing letters and numbers.

Trace the dotted line to help the bees get to the flowers. Can you buzz like a bee?

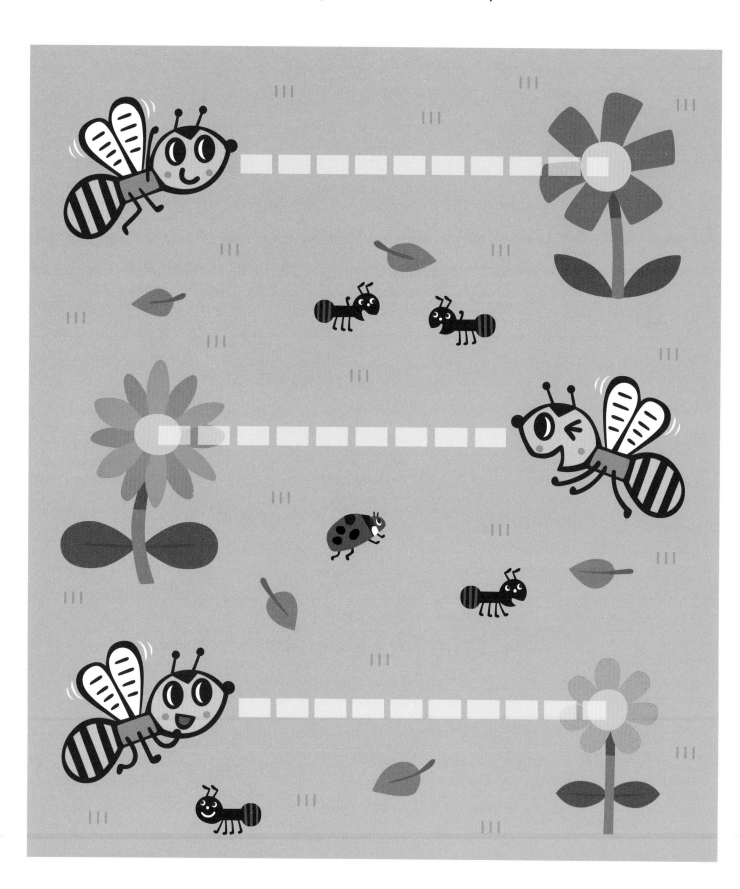

Let's Draw Horizontal Lines

To Parents: Unlike in the previous activity, there are no dotted lines to trace. Encourage your child to draw slowly. Some children may not stay inside the white area, and that is okay. With practice, their drawing will improve.

Draw lines from ⭐ to ⬤ to help the crabs walk across the beach.

Let's Draw Diagonal Lines

To Parents: In this activity, your child will practice drawing diagonal lines. It is okay if your child strays away from the gray line, but encourage him or her to keep trying.

Trace the lines from ★ to ●.

Let's Draw Diagonal Lines

To Parents: The diagonal lines in this activity move in different directions. Make sure your child sees the beginning and end point of each line before he or she starts drawing.

GOOD JOB!

Sticker

Draw lines from ★ to ● to help the pandas reach their friends.

Let's Trace Shooting Stars

To Parents: The diagonal lines in this activity are long. Encourage your child to draw slowly. It will help him or her stay on the gray guiding line.

GOOD JOB!

Sticker

Trace the lines from to ⬤.

Let's Draw the Pig's Path

To Parents: One of the diagonal paths below has a gray line for your child to trace. The others do not. It is okay if your child's line is not straight or if it veers out of the white path. Line-drawing skills will improve with practice.

Sticker

Draw lines from ⭐ to ●. Place the pig stickers on the .

Let's Draw Rain

To Parents: This activity focuses on both creativity and handwriting skills. Encourage your child to draw lines and raindrops anywhere on the blue background.

Frog and Snail are playing in the rain. Can you draw more rain?

Let's Match the Puppies

To Parents: Point to the top picture. Ask, "What animal is this?" Then ask, "Which other picture shows the same animal?" Have your child trace the path to the matching picture with his or her finger first. Then have your child draw the path with a crayon.

GOOD JOB!

Sticker

Draw a line from the puppy to its match.

Let's Match the Animals

To Parents: Help your child identify the match first, then trace and draw the correct path.

Help the animals find their match! Draw a line from one rabbit to the other rabbit. Draw a line from one panda to the other panda.

Let's Match the Animals

To Parents: Have your child identify all the animals before he or she begins. Not only will it help your child locate the matches, it will also build vocabulary.

Draw a line from each animal to its match.

Let's Match the Birds

To Parents: All the animals below are birds. Talk with your child about the color and shape of each bird. Help her or him recognize the differences. Then guide your child to trace and draw the paths between each matching pair of birds.

GOOD JOB!
Sticker

Draw a line from each bird to its match. Chirp like a bird when you are done!

Let's Draw Grass

To Parents: First, help your child choose the correct color crayon for the grass. After he or she finishes drawing the grass, ask, "How many rabbits are in the picture?" "How many birds are flying in the sky?"

The rabbits are hopping in the field. Draw more grass for them to hop in.

Let's Trace a Line That Bends

To Parents: This activity boosts fine motor control and builds handwriting skills. Encourage your child to stop fully before changing directions.

GOOD JOB!

Sticker

Trace the line from ⭐ to ⚫.

Let's Draw Lines That Change Direction

To Parents: Drawing lines that change direction helps build fine motor control and handwriting skills. Encourage your child to stop at each corner before changing direction.

Sticker

Draw each line from ⭐ to ⬤. Try to stay on the white path.

Let's Draw Lines That Change Direction

To Parents: This activity focuses on drawing straight lines that change direction. This can be difficult. Encourage your child to work slowly and to pause at each corner before making the sharp turn.

GOOD JOB!
Sticker

Trace each line from ⭐ to ⬤.

Let's Help the Fish Swim Along the Path

To Parents: Say, "Look at the blue fish. Can you help it swim along the path?" Then have your child draw a line along the path. Ask your child to help the pink, green, and yellow fish, too.

GOOD JOB!

Sticker

Draw a line in each path from to ●.

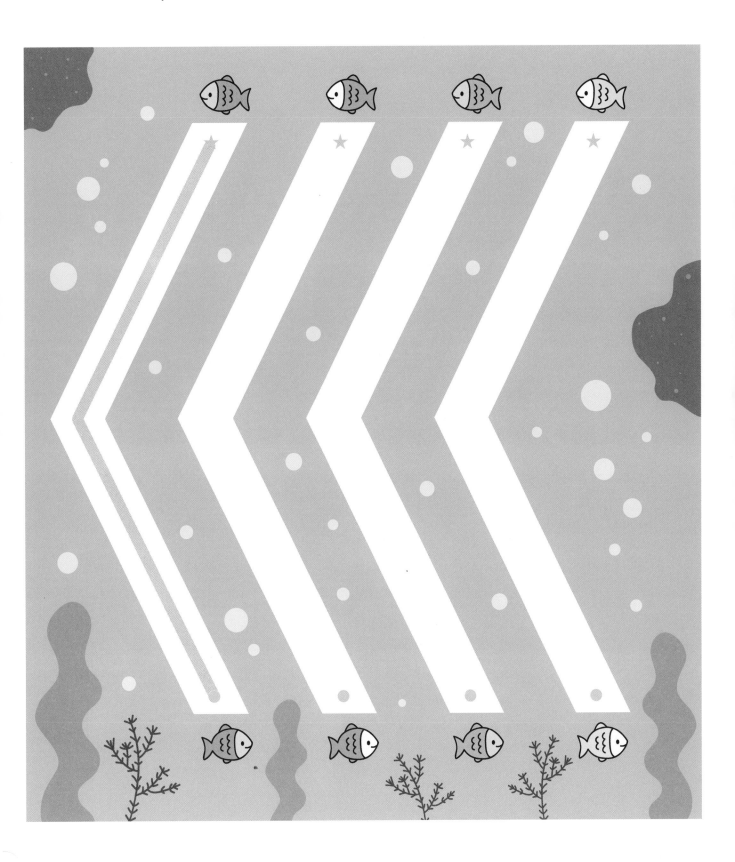

Let's Draw Zigzags

To Parents: This activity focuses on drawing zigzag lines from left to right. Encourage your child to trace the lines with a finger first. Tracing and drawing promote hand-eye coordination and fine motor control.

Trace the zigzags from ★ to ●.

Let's Make the Rabbits Hop

To Parents: Ask, "How does the rabbit get to the carrot?" As your child draws the zigzags, encourage him or her to say, "Hop, hop, hop."

GOOD JOB!
Sticker

Help the rabbits get their carrots. Draw a line in each path from ★ to ●.
Before drawing the last line, place the rabbit sticker on the 🐰 .

Let's Follow the Fish

To Parents: In this activity, your child will draw a whole path made of zigzags. After your child has completed the maze, ask questions about the different shells, creatures, and colors in the picture.

GOOD JOB!

Sticker

Draw a path from to to make the fish swim to the bottom of the ocean.

Let's Follow the Birds

To Parents: This activity is designed to teach how to draw arcs, a skill needed when writing numbers and letters.

GOOD JOB!

Sticker

Draw a line in each path from ⭐ to ●.

Let's Draw Curves

To Parents: This is practice for drawing curved lines. Drawing curves helps children learn how to form letters and numbers. When your child is done, show him or her your best fish face. Ask, "Can you make a fish face, too?"

Draw a line in each path from ⭐ to ⬤ to make the fish swim.

Let's Draw Curved Lines

To Parents: In this activity, your child will practice drawing curved lines. This is an important handwriting skill.

The animals are swimming! Draw a line in each white path from ● to ● to catch up.

Let's Draw Curves

To Parents: In order to draw letters and numbers, children will need to know how to draw straight lines and curved lines. This exercise is good practice for drawing curved lines.

The worms are racing across the grass. Draw a line in each white path from ⭐ to ⬤.

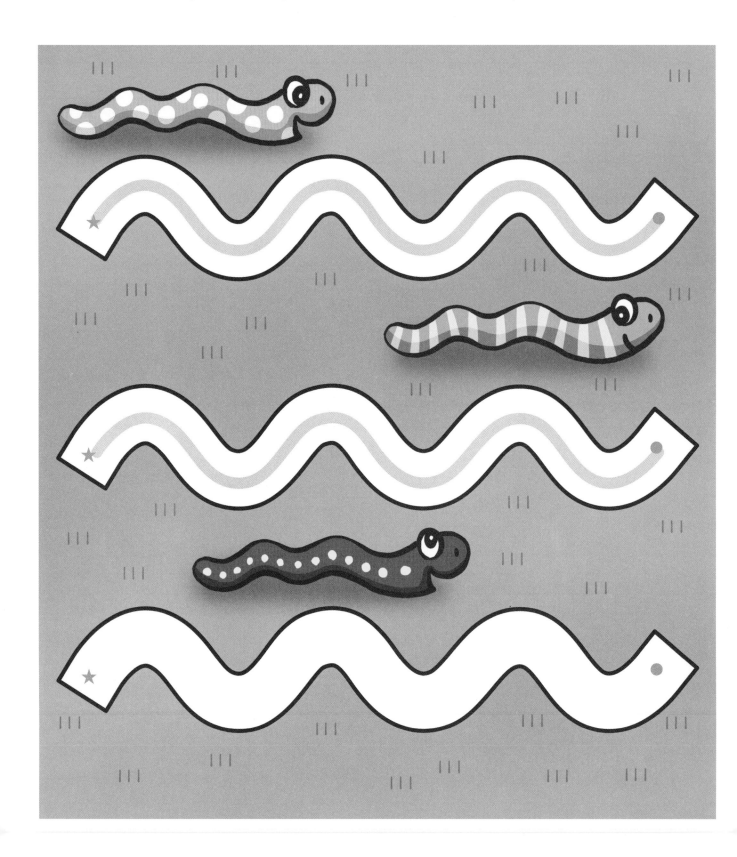

Let's Trace Curves

To Parents: The curves in the lines below are smaller and tighter than the ones in the last activity. Encourage your child to trace the lines with a finger first to practice the motion.

Draw the lines in each path from ★ to ●.

Let's Go to the Picnic

To Parents: This maze goes from the bottom to the top of the page. Make sure your child knows where the start of the maze is. Then ask a fun question, like, "What do you think the kangaroos will eat at their picnic?"

Draw a path through the maze from from ➡ to ➡.

Let's Find the Number in the Chicken

To Parents: This activity exercises your child's number-recognition and coloring skills. Your child can also color in the chicken, if he or she wants to.

GOOD JOB!

Sticker

Find the number TWO **2** and color it using any color you like.

Let's Trace and Write Numbers

To Parents: Have your child trace the number with his or her finger first. Then, your child can practice with a crayon. Show your child that there are two chicks on the page.

Trace the number TWO **2** with your finger.

Trace the number TWO **2** with a crayon.

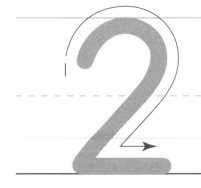

Let's Find the Elephant

To Parents: On this page, your child will work on connecting words and objects. If your child has never seen an elephant before, explain some characteristics of an elephant that will help. You can also look up photos of elephants to share.

GOOD JOB!

Sticker

Draw a circle around the elephant.

Let's Draw Seeds

To Parents: Encourage your child to draw as many seeds as he or she wants. Engage your child by asking, "What kinds of flowers do you think will grow from these seeds?"

Draw seeds in the garden to make flowers grow.

Let's Follow the Frog's Path

To Parents: Drawing connected arcs will help prepare your child for drawing letters. Ask your child if he or she has ever seen a frog. Ask what sound a frog makes.

Draw lines from ⭐ to ⬤ to make the frogs jump. How many frogs do you see?

Let's Follow the Rabbits

To Parents: Here, your child will practice drawing arcs. In the second and third paths, there is no gray guideline. Encourage your child to take his or her time. It is easier to draw carefully when drawing slowly.

GOOD JOB!

Sticker

The rabbits are hopping across the grass. Draw a line in each path from ★ to ●.

Let's Get to the Cake

To Parents: Encourage your child to draw slowly to keep from bumping into the grass. But it is okay if he or she goes outside the white area.

Draw a path through the maze from from ➡ to ➡.

Let's Help the Frogs Jump

To Parents: In this activity, your child will practice drawing a series of consecutive arcs. Make sure your child stops at the end of each arc before moving on to the next.

Trace the line of the jumping frog from ★ to ●. Can you find a turtle on the page?

Let's Draw Arcs

To Parents: This activity focuses on drawing lines with multiple arcs. Offer encouragement as your child draws the sheep's wool by saying, "Those arcs are great!"

Draw a line in each white path from ● to ●.

Let's Find the Number in the Butterfly

To Parents: This activity exercises number-recognition and coloring skills. After coloring the number 3, ask your child if there are any groups of three on the page (for example, three clouds or three dots on the butterfly's wing). If your child does not spot them, point them out and count together.

GOOD JOB!

Sticker

Find the number ^{THREE} 3 and color it using any color you like.

Let's Trace and Write Numbers

To Parents: On this page, your child will practice writing numbers. Have your child trace the number with his or her finger first. Then, your child can practice with a crayon.

Trace the number ^{THREE} 3 with your finger.

Trace the number ^{THREE} 3 with a crayon.

Let's Trace Spirals

To Parents: Have your child trace the line with his or her finger before moving on to tracing it with a crayon or thick marker. For this exercise, have your child start at the inside and work outward.

GOOD JOB!

Sticker

Trace the spiral in each sheep's coat from ★ to ●. What does a sheep say?

Let's Draw Spirals

To Parents: In this activity, your child will practice drawing spirals, starting from the outside and moving inward.

Draw a line in each path from ⭐ to ⚫.

Let's Find the Giraffes

To Parents: Guide your child to identify the giraffes. Explain that he or she should draw a circle around each giraffe, rather than one big circle around both of them.

Draw a circle around each giraffe.

Let's Find the Birds

To Parents: The circles around the objects do not need to be neat. It is more important for your child to determine which objects should be circled and which should not be circled.

Draw a circle around each bird.

Let's Find the Fish

Draw a circle around each fish.

Let's Trace the Dragonfly's Path

To Parents: In this activity, your child will practice drawing a line that crosses over itself. It may be confusing at first. That's okay. Soon, drawing loops will be fun.

GOOD JOB!
Sticker

Trace the lines in each path from ★ to ●. Then, place the dragonfly sticker on the ✦.

Let's Draw Loops

To Parents: Make sure your child looks for the arrows before drawing.
The arrows show which way the lines should go.

The butterflies are making loops. Draw a line in each path from ★ to ●.

Let's Draw the Bee's Path

To Parents: Here your child will practice drawing one long, looping line. Make sure your child pays attention to the blue arrows throughout the maze so he or she knows which way to draw the loops.

Draw a path from ➡ to ⬇ to make the bee fly through the air.
Put the bee sticker at the end of the line.

Let's Go Through the Maze

To Parents: In this maze, one path leads to the party and two lead to dead ends. It is important for your child to stop and look at each path option before deciding which way to go.

It's Mama Mole's birthday. Draw a path from ➡ to ➡ to get Papa Mole to the party.

Let's Find the Crabs

To Parents: This activity is designed to exercise your child's observational skills. For extra fun, make crab claws with your hands.

Draw one circle around all the crabs.

Let's Find the Butterflies

Draw one circle around all the butterflies.

Let's Find the Dogs

To Parents: This activity is intended to enhance your child's ability to identify objects in a group. Make sure your child draws only one circle, as the directions say to do.

GOOD JOB!

Sticker

Draw one circle around all the dogs.

Let's Count the Squirrels

To Parents: After your child places the correct number of squirrel stickers in the box below, extend the activity by having him or her count the birds.

Sticker

Count the squirrels. Then, place the same number of  stickers in the ☐ at the bottom of the page.

Let's Connect the Dots

To Parents: First, count to 3 with your child. Then, explain that it is important to connect the dots in order to see the picture.

Connect the ● from **ONE** **1** ➡ **TWO** **2** ➡ **THREE** **3** with a line.

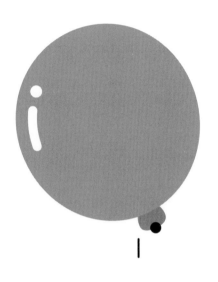

Let's Go Underground

To Parents: In this maze, your child will practice drawing a long curvy line as she or he moves through an ant's nest. Ask your child questions, such as "How many ants do you see?" and "Where are the worms?"

Draw a path from ⬇ to ⬅.

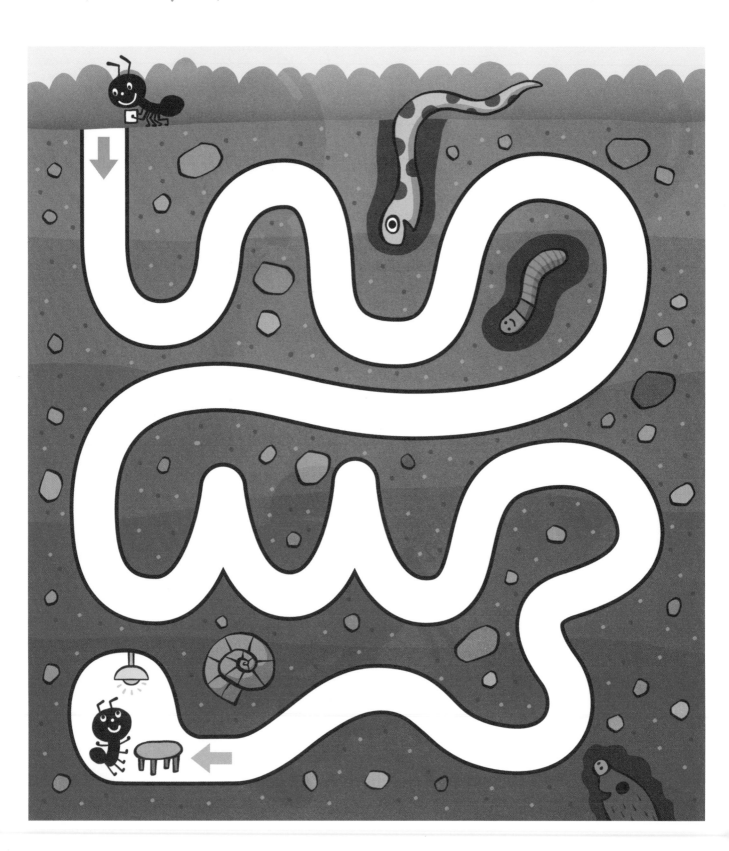

Let's Help the Bear

To Parents: This is a fun maze for practicing arcs and curvy lines. Encourage your child to draw slowly to avoid going outside the path.

Bear wants to visit his friend Rabbit. Place the Rabbit sticker at the end of the maze.
Then, draw a path from ⬅ to ➡ to help Bear reach his friend.

Let's Count the Pandas

To Parents: Let your child choose a color to fill in the circle or circles at the bottom of the page. It is a simple way to excercise creativity and decision-making skills.

GOOD JOB!

Sticker

Count the pandas. Then, color the same amount of ◯ at the bottom.

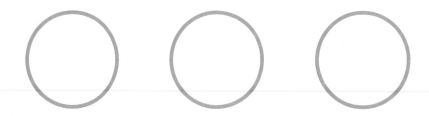

Let's Count the Elephants

To Parents: After your child has finished counting and coloring the circles at the bottom, extend the fun by asking if he or she can imitate an elephant.

Count the elephants. Then, color the same amount of ◯ at the bottom.

Let's Count the Zebras

To Parents: Your child may get confused because the zebras are different sizes. Explain that the size of the zebras does not matter.

Count the zebras. Then, color the same amount of ◯ at the bottom.

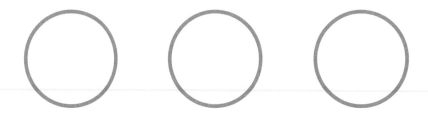

Let's Draw the Paths

To Parents: For each picture below, make sure your child knows where to start. Encourage her or him to draw each outline in one stroke. Praise your child for drawing neat lines.

Draw the outline of the shapes below. Draw a line in each path from ☆ to ●.

Let's Draw the Squirrel

To Parents: This activity incorporates all the different lines your child learned how to draw in this book. Encourage your child to pause when changing direction to improve fine motor control.

Let's draw the shape of the squirrel. Follow the path from ★ to ●.